The Way Things Were

BONNIE
SCOTLAND

Andrew Pagett

Illustrated by Victorian Illustrators

BROCKHAMPTON PRESS

Ye flowery banks o' bonnie Doon,
How can ye bloom sae fair;
How can ye chant, ye little birds,
And I sae fu' o' care?

Robert Burns, *The Banks of Doon*

Bonnie Scotland

First published by Brockhampton Press Ltd
20 Bloomsbury Street
London WC1B 3QA

© Brockhampton Press Ltd, 1999

ISBN 1 86019 939 9

Victorian watercolours reproduced by permission.
Every effort has been made to trace the copyright holders.
The editor apologizes for any omissions which may
have occurred.

Conceived and designed by Savitri Books Ltd

Printed and bound by
APP Printing, Singapore

CONTENTS

✦

✦

INTRODUCTION

Scotland in the early years of the twentieth century was, as it is today, a land of infinite variety and contrast. In Glasgow, ship-building and commerce thrived; in Edinburgh old glories from the days when the country was ruled from here were fading slowly. And in the north, in the untameable Highlands and on the islands which only the most intrepid tourist chose to penetrate, 'civilisation' and the calming influence of the Protestant church were newcomers, fighting centuries of tradition in which clan warfare and subsistence living had played strong parts.

This book cannot pretend to be a complete portrait of such a complex and diverse country. Rather, it selects from the work of a number of artists of the period, who painted the landscapes, townscapes and people they knew and loved. Many of the pictures included here show mountains and glens as unspoiled now as they were then; others recall a way of life that has all but vanished. Buildings in ruins reflect the turbulence that seems always to have been a part of Scottish history – conflicts between Scots and Norsemen, Scots and English, Protestants and Catholics, and perhaps most devastatingly Scots and other Scots.

The text is drawn largely from the writings of Scottish travellers working at the same period as the artists. They show that through the centuries of upheaval and bloodshed, there has run in the Scottish character a thread of steadfastness, courage, piety and devotion to the cause each individual has seen as right. They also convey a love of the landscape that only those born to it can truly feel, but that other fortunate observers may be permitted to share.

Opposite:

SPRING IN A BIRCH-WOOD NEAR LOCH MAREE

EDINBURGH

Any tour of Scotland must begin with its capital, and any sketch of Edinburgh must begin, almost of necessity, with the castle, because it stands at the head, even as Holyrood stands at the foot, of that 'hog's back ridge' on which Edinburgh is situated.

The view from Castlehill is exquisite, but as one passes along the Esplanade, a favourite promenade for the Edinburgh citizens in the seventeenth and eighteenth centuries, one is struck by other memories. For this is the site that witnessed the many executions for witchcraft which stained the castle's history for over 200 years. It is said that during this period no fewer than 2000 people met their death here, with as many as a dozen at a time strangled and burned, often for the most trivial offences. One of the most notorious of these miscarriages of justice concerned the young and beautiful Lady Jane Douglas, widow of John, Lord Glamis, who was falsely accused by a rejected suitor of conspiring to murder the king through sorcery.

To enter the castle itself, one turns from the Esplanade and crosses the old moat. A massive gateway of great antiquity, studded with iron bolts, and a nearby guardhouse were the first line of defence when the Castle was truly a fortress. Under the archway called the Portcullis Gate the slit in which the pronged portcullis once hung can still be discerned. Inside this arch is the platform on which sits the great cannon known as Mons Meg. The cannon has played a great and varied part in the history of the Castle, taking part in the siege of Dumbarton in 1489 and in the celebrations of the marriage of Mary Queen of Scots to the Dauphin of France in 1558. It burst in 1682

Opposite:

Edinburgh castle from the West Kirk

while firing a salute to the Duke of York, was removed to the Tower of London in 1745 and restored to Edinburgh in 1829 through the influence of Sir Walter Scott.

Next to this great emblem of war stands the oldest and probably the smallest place of worship now standing in Scotland. St Margaret's Chapel measures a mere 16 feet in length by 10 in width. Its exact age is not known, but its architecture is Early Norman with some Saxon features adn it is thought to have been founded by another Margaret, the English consort of Malcolm. Canmore, who succeeded Macbeth as king in 1057. According to tradition it is here that King Edward I of England (1272–1307) – the so-called 'Hammer of the Scots' – accepted the oaths of loyalty of the Abbot of Holyrood and other Scottish ecclesiastics.

Perhaps the greatest attraction for most visitors to the Castle is the Regalia of Scotland – the crown, sceptre and sword of state, the oldest Crown Jewels in Europe. These are housed in the rather gloomy Crown Room, guarded by two doors of immense strength and behind a heavy iron grating. Some antiquarians believe that the Crown dates back as far as Robert the Bruce (1306–29). Certainly all the Regalia suffered many vicissitudes before coming to rest in their present safe home. During the time of Cromwell they were hidden under the pulpit of a distant church; when the Kingdoms of England and Scotland were united, the Scots hid their Crown Jewels away in a sealed chamber, where they remained for 110 years, believed by many to be lost forever. Again, it was thanks to the efforts of Sir Walter Scott that they were discovered and placed on display.

To set out on a circular tour of historic Edinburgh, from the Castle to the Palace of Holyrood via the Royal Mile and returning via Princes Street, one

Opposite:

Castle Hill

leaves the Castle via the Esplanade and Castlehill to pass through the area dedicated to the memory of the pastoral poet Allan Ramsay (1686–1758). Ramsay's most famous work, *The Gentle Shepherd*, seems oversentimental today, but posterity owes him a debt of gratitude for rediscovering and preserving many ancient and dying Scottish songs and ballads.

The Ramsays were a distinguished family: the poet's son, also Allan, was a talented artist who became official portrait painter to the English King George III, and Sir Andrew Ramsay, Chief Magistrate of Edinburgh for no fewer than sixteen years, was the first to have the title of Lord Provost (equivalent to the English Lord Mayor) conferred on him.

Passing on down the Lawnmarket, where the 'lawn' or cloth merchants used to sell their wares, one comes in a few minutes to the Parliament House on the fringes of the Old Town. Parliament Square stands on what was once the principal burial ground of the area, but after 1574 no further burials took place here and in 1632 the Great Hall of the Parliament House was erected on the site. A nineteenth-century writer describes how it was in his time:

> From then on the 'Estates of the Realm', as the Scottish Parliament was known, met here, and around this centre gradually arose the 'towering lands', containing the flats and apartments that housed judges, lawyers, clergy, leading merchants and others whose professions demanded that they live in the middle of town. Now that the building is no longer used for the purposes of government, it is likely to be filled most days of the week with gowned and wigged advocates pacing up and down its length, either in consultation with clients and their solicitors, or in animated conversation with their peers.

Opposite:

RAMSAY GARDEN

The Great Hall is indeed a noble one, measuring 122 feet long by 49 wide, but what strikes one most of all is the lofty open roof, 60 feet high, formed of dark oak beams with cross-braces and hammer-beams resting on curiously carved corbels. There are three fireplaces on the west side of the hall, all beautifully decorated; the central one is a fine example of wood carving in the old Italian style, the middle panel of which contains a representation of St Peter being presented with the Keys of the Kingdom of Heaven.

But unquestionably the object which at once arrests the attention of the visitor is the great stained-glass window at the southern end of the hall. Placed in its present position in 1868, it is a fine specimen of German art, having been designed by Wilhelm von Kaulbach and executed by the Chevalier Ainmuller of Munich. It depicts the Institution of the Courts of Session by King James V in 1532. Originally held in the old Low Council House in the Tolbooth, the Courts of Session, the highest judicial tribunal in Scotland, are to this day held in chambers adjacent to the Great Hall. The central figure in the window is, of course, the King. His mother, Margaret of England, sits on the right of the throne, while the figure represented reading the Charter of Creation is Alexander Myln, Abbot of Cambuskenneth, Lord President of the Court.

Many fine statues and busts, also numerous rare portraits of deceased judges and jurists are ranged along and hung upon the walls. The four windows on the west side of the hall are filled in with the heraldic bearings of various eminent lawyers, placed there in 1870 to decorate the hall.

Opposite:

PARLIAMENT HOUSE

Before leaving the hall it is worth turning to look back once more on the ever-changing picture. How various have been the scenes whereon the grand old roof has looked since the days when the Scottish Parliament met here, down through those times when booths and stalls were allowed within the precincts of the hall, and when two judges actually held their courts in it, hearing cases amid the turmoil and babel of tongues which prevailed around.

From Parliament Square it is easy to stroll up to the Old Town, where are to be found the Greyfriars' Kirk and Heriot's Hospital. The hospital is a magnificent structure, begun in 1628 under the terms of the will of George Heriot, alias 'Jingling Geordie', the most famous goldsmith, banker and jeweller in the annals of that craft in Edinburgh. His booth, which stood in the Tolbooth, measured only 7 feet square, but his name on the lintel was still legible when the structure was swept away in the early years of the nineteenth century.

Heriot was goldsmith to King James VI (James I of England) and his consort Anne of Denmark and, when his exchequer ran low, the King was not above visiting the goldsmith and requesting the loan of a few thousand pounds. One day, 'Geordie', on being summoned to Holyrood Palace, found His Majesty sitting before a fire of logs containing aromatic gums, which diffused a pleasant fragrance throughout the room. On Heriot remarking upon the agreeable odour, the king replied that it was as costly as it was pleasant. To this the goldsmith replied that if James would visit him at his workshop, he would show him a still costlier fire. The king agreed and the next day proceeded to the goldsmith's booth. To his surprise, he saw nothing but an ordinary coal fire.

'Why, Master Heriot, this is not so costly a fire as mine!' he exclaimed.

Opposite:

VIEW OF THE OLD TOWN

'Wait, Your Majesty, until I get the fuel,' said Heriot, who thereupon went to his money-chest, brought out a bond for £2000 which he had lent to James and laid it on the coals. The devious monarch waited until the flames had consumed it and then said, 'In truth, Geordie, yours is the costlier blaze.'

So indispensable was the goldsmith to James that he eventually followed the King to London, but he was always devoted to his native town and the noble hospital that bears his name is proof of the fact.

The first King James of Scotland founded the monastery of the Greyfriars, which stood on the site of the present churchyard, in 1429; so rich and splendid was it that the Burgundian princess Mary of Gueldres lodged there prior to her marriage to James II. Henry VI of England sought refuge there with his wife and son when the course of the Wars of the Roses ran against him, and the schools too enjoyed a high reputation. The monastery was destroyed in a fit of anti-Catholic zeal during the Reformation in 1558 and, under the auspices of Mary Queen of Scots, the site briefly became the burial place of those who had died of the plague. Happily, the building of what is now called the Old Greyfriars Kirk in 1612 restored the area to some of its former esteem.

Heading back past Parliament House, one reaches the Cathedral of St Giles, the original parish church of Edinburgh. Externally, it appears a modern Gothic structure with choir, nave and transepts; but it is in reality very old. Its history can be traced from the early part of the twelfth century, when it seems to have superseded an edifice of a still earlier date. The original pillars of this twelfth-century building are still intact; the crown-shaped spire and some of the columns inside may also date from this period, but the rest of the structure was erected and extended at various times.

Opposite:

THE INTERIOR OF ST GILES CATHEDRAL

Continuing eastwards towards the Royal Mile and the Palace of Holyrood, one passes the North Bridge, one of the landmarks of the New Town. This development was first projected in 1752 as a way of extending the city and thus solving the increasing problems of overcrowding. A feature of the scheme was to be the draining of the 'Nor' Loch', an artificial sheet of water below Castle Rock and the ridge on which the Old Town stands, which had in ancient times been marsh, but as early as the twelfth century had been drained and converted into a pleasure garden, then flooded again in order to enhance the security of the town in the troubled reign of James II. Once the loch was drained, according to the eighteenth-century plan, a huge bridge would be thrown across the broad ravine to join the Old Town with the New.

In fact, a bridge across the Nor' Loch had been discussed many times before it became a reality – Sir William Bruce of Kinross, Scottish architect to Charles II, had first planned one nearly a hundred years earlier. Even when the design was accepted, in 1752, there were further delays; no steps appear to have been taken to further the project for seven years, and then the Town Council had to apply to Parliament for a bill to extend the 'royalty' of the city over the ground where the New Town stands today. When no bill was forthcoming for four years, the Lord Provost, George Drummond, persuaded the Council to begin work without official authorisation.

On 21 October 1763, therefore, the foundation of the North Bridge was laid with great pomp and ceremony by Drummond, but the structure was not finished until 1772, an unfortunate landslip causing the fall of a part of the southern end and delaying the completion of the work.

The increasing demands of traffic led to the bridge being widened in 1873, but by the last years of the nineteenth century congestion in Edinburgh was

Opposite:

NORTH BRIDGE

such that an entirely new bridge was needed. The old structure was demolished, and a wholly new North Bridge opened in 1900.

Passing by rather than across the bridge, one reaches what is known as John Knox's house. There is no firm evidence that the great Protestant reformer actually lived here, but tradition is strong.

John Knox was a disciple of the earlier Lutheran reformer George Wishart, who was burned for his beliefs under the orders of Cardinal Beaton, Archbishop of St Andrews, in 1546. Beaton was assassinated three months later, and his murderers took possession of St Andrews Castle, where Knox joined them and was ordained as a minister. After the castle was captured by the French Knox spent four years as a galley slave, then returned to England, where he found favour at the court of the Protestant Edward VI and worked with Archbishop Cranmer on revisions to *The Book of Common Prayer*. When Edward died and was succeeded by his fervently Catholic sister Mary, Knox fled again to Europe, where he met and was strongly influenced by Calvin. In this period he wrote his famous pamphlet *First Blast of the Trumpet Against the Monstrous Regiment of Women* (of which it has been said that the title is the most interesting part), deploring the influence on England of Queen Mary and on Scotland of another equally staunch Catholic, the Frenchwoman Mary of Guise, regent during the minority of her daughter, Mary Queen of Scots.

The late 1550s found Knox back in Scotland, preaching against the abuses and immorality in the Catholic Church in Rome and converting many to his cause. It is largely through his influence that Protestantism became established in Scotland, though he never succeeded in persuading his own Queen to his point of view.

Opposite:

JOHN KNOX'S HOUSE

The irregular architecture of his house on the High Street, the peaked French windows, outside stair and projecting gables, prove it to belong to the middle of the sixteenth century, though it bears the date 1490. Over its west front runs the inscription 'Lufe God above al and zour Nichbour as zourself'. On the outside of the house a stair leads from the street into the audience hall, now fitted up as a museum. The window in this hall is called the 'preaching window', tradition having it that Knox was in the habit of standing here and addressing the people below. From this room a circular stair leads into the bedchamber where he probably died in 1572. A plaque said to mark his grave is set into the causeway outside the Parliament House.

And so one continues down the Royal Mile and the Canongate to the Palace of Holyrood House, where John Knox must often have walked on his way to preach his unproductive sermons to Mary Queen of Scots. Although the palace will always be most closely associated with this tragic Queen, the site whereon it stands at the eastern end of the city was first endowed as an Abbey some 400 years earlier, in the reign of King David I, known as St David (1124–53).

The Abbey itself is now a ruin, with little remaining but a weather-stained facade and a shattered arch, but, as one writer puts it:

> In its time it has witnessed more of the joy and sorrow, marriage and funeral, gay levee and ghastly tragedy, of the wealth and woe alike of Scotland's kings and Scotland's capital than any other building – except perhaps the imposing fortress at the other end of the town.

Even though one can admire the noble lines of the chapel, it is worth bearing in mind that what remains is only the nave of the original structure. The proportions of the building must once have been exceedingly imposing; again and again we read of 'the magnificent Abbey-Kirk of Halirude'.

SUNRISE OVER EDINBURGH

As one's gaze travels along the line of noble pillars which divides the nave from the aisles, it rests almost inevitably on the great window, which occupied nearly the whole of the eastern end of the church. It is 34 feet high by 20 wide, and was built after the choir and transepts had been demolished by the English. The eastern ends of the aisles were, subsequent to the Reformation, filled in with windows in order that the structure might be used as a Chapel Royal. The south side or southern aisle remains in the best state of preservation, or perhaps has been most artistically restored. The roof of the aisle and the pillars still remain, with various arches and some fragments of the upper storey.

The wall of the northern aisle is supported on the outside by seven flying buttresses adorned with canopied niches and pinnacles, while the doorway at the western end of this aisle is rich in ornament, but the style is at least 200 years later than that of the other parts.

Within the enclosure of the Abbey many distinguished persons are interred, although the Royal Vault was violated by an infuriated mob during the Revolution of 1688 and the coffins therein wantonly destroyed. Records show that, among many others, James V and his first Queen, Magdalene, were buried there, as was Mary Queen of Scots's second husband, Lord Darnley, until his son, by then King James VI of Scotland and I of England, ordered that his father's body be brought to England and interred in Westminster Abbey.

In the beautiful grounds to the west of the Abbey may be seen Queen Mary's Dial, a remarkable old time-piece, and a quaint little building known as Queen Mary's Bath, in which tradition has it that the Queen used to bathe in white wine to enhance her beauty.

Opposite:

CHAPEL ROYAL, HOLYROOD RUIN

The building of Holyrood House was begun by James II, to provide Edinburgh with a palace whither he could take his Queen ,without her being brought into contact with the 'rough and coarse soldiery' who formed the garrison at the castle. Although the greater part of the more ancient portion of the palace was altered and renewed fifty years later, when James' grandson James IV brought his bride, Margaret of England, there, there is no question that it was begun by the earlier monarch and further enlarged by his son, James III. Although modernised by Charles II and James II (of England) in the seventeenth century, for the greater part of this section was injured by fire in the time of Cromwell (who was using the palace as a barracks), there are still some remains of the ancient residence of the earlier Jameses visible to indicate its age.

A private stair leading up from one of the palace's many courtyards takes one to Queen Mary's apartment. By this staircase the assassins of Mary's secretary Rizzio gained admission to the apartments of Lord Darnley, and were led by him to the Queen's supper room where the unfortunate victim was to be found, sitting with Her Majesty and one or two friends. Darnley and his fellow conspirators dragged Rizzio from the room, through the Queen's bedroom and audience chamber, to the head of the principal staircase where their murderous work was completed. Rizzio's blood soaked into the flooring, where the stain is still shown. The partition which now encloses the spot is said to have been erected by order of Mary so that she could not see the marks, though she would not permit them to be obliterated,

Opposite:

MARIE DE LORRAINE, QUEEN OF JAMES V, AND MOTHER OF
MARY QUEEN OF SCOTS

wishing that they should remain as a memorial and confirm her revenge.

Few historians believe it is a coincidence that Darnley himself was assassinated within a year of this foul deed; most maintain that the second murder was perpetrated by the Queen's future husband, the Earl of Bothwell, of whom we shall hear more later in this book.

On leaving Holyrood, one passes down Calton Hill to the thoroughfare many now consider the centre of Edinburgh, Princes Street. Laid out at the time of the development of the New Town, it was first to be called St Giles Street, but King George III protested on the grounds that the St Giles area of London had such an unsavoury reputation that the name would suggest to any Londoner who heard it 'all that was mean and squalid'. So Princes Street it became, and it has been aptly styled 'the noblest street in Europe'. One commentator, writing in the early years of the twentieth century, described it thus:

> For variety and richness of scenery, for picturesqueness of situation, for magnificence of architectural effects, it is unrivalled. Yet as recently as the early eighteenth century, all the surface now covered with streets of houses, the stones of which are already beginning to assume the tinge of antiquity, was a wide expanse of cornfields and dairy meadows, where the citizens went to enjoy a country walk or to eat curds and cream at Bearford's Park or Wood's Farm. Where East and West Princes Street are today was the sedge-fringed Nor' Loch, famed for its mammoth eels and its innumerable waterfowl.

Princes Street, save at its eastern end, was at first wholly devoted

Opposite:

PRINCES STREET AND SCOTT MONUMENT

to residential purposes, but after 1830 business premises began to banish the mansions, and now the magnificent thoroughfare is mainly occupied by the best hotels and the finest shops in the city. The architecture has been carefully watched, and no structure of a low elevation or of a type out of harmony with the prevailing character and symmetry of the whole has been permitted to be erected.

The most familiar feature of this part of Edinburgh is the 200-foot high Scott Monument in Princes Street Gardens. It was erected in 1844 in memory of the writer Sir Walter Scott who, though much associated with the Border Country, was also, as we have seen, active in the interests of his capital city. The monument cost £15,500, which substantial sum was raised wholly by public subscription. It takes the form of a large open Gothic pinnacle 200 feet high, the central spire resting on four arches which form a canopy over the figure of the novelist, seated with a shepherd's plaid thrown around him and with his favourite staghound, Maida, at his feet. The design was originally prepared by a young, self-taught artist named Kemp, who tragically drowned before the work could be completed. The statue itself was executed in Carrara marble by Sir John Steell and is generally deemed 'marvellously lifelike and true to nature'. All over the monument are niches filled with statuettes of the characters from Scott's Waverley novels, while the capitals of the pilasters supporting the vaulted roof are ornamented by likenesses of other celebrated Scottish writers, including Robert Burns, Allan Ramsay and Lord Byron.

To complete the circuit by returning to the Castle, one must now pass two intriguing buildings situated at the lower end of the Mound, a vast but ugly accumulation of earth bisecting the valley, which owes its origins to the earth

Opposite:

THE ROYAL INSTITUTION

thrown out when the foundations of the New Town were being dug. Both these buildings are constructed after the model of Greek temples and were designed by the Scottish architect William Playfair. The first is the Royal Institution, founded in 1823, a fine example of pure Doric architecture. Eight sphinxes adorn the four corners of the roof, while behind the apex of the northern portico is a colossal crowned statue by Steell of Queen Victoria, clad in state robes and bearing the orb and sceptre in her hand.

The other building, whose foundation stone was laid by Prince Albert in 1850, houses the Scottish Art Galleries. Its style is Ionic, and the north and south ends are decorated by exquisitely symmetrical Ionic porticos. While its contents cannot compare with the great collections of London and the Continent, it nevertheless includes fine examples of the work of Tintoretto, Rembrandt, Rubens, van Eyck, Veronese, Velazquez and many others, along with the best work of Scottish artists such as 'the Scottish Vandyke', George Jamesone (1586–1650). The nickname arose because he was believed at one time to have studied in Antwerp under Rubens. This is now known not to be true; Jamesone is recorded instead as having been apprenticed to a largely forgotten Edinburgh painter named John Anderson, but the epithet has never been abandoned.

Such then are a few of the principal sites of this great capital. Nor it the area's greatness confined to the city itself. There is also much to see in the region immediately surrounding Edinburgh.

Opposite:

NIGHT-TIME VIEW – AYONT THE TWAL

THE ENVIRONS OF EDINBURGH

The first port of call on leaving the capital is Roslin, situated in one of the loveliest vales in the country. It increases in loveliness the higher one goes, for the surroundings of the 'Scottish Arno', as the northern stretch of the River Esk has been called, are, according to one commentator, 'as picturesquely beautiful as they are exquisitely varied'.

> The rugged grandeur of cliff and lichened rock, of foaming cascade and eddying linn is succeeded by rich diversity and vivid contrasts of colour in the marvellously tinted foliage. Flowery banks and grassy knolls, fairy meads and daisied holm succeed the darkling forest depths, where the eye endowed with fancy's vision gazes down the forest boles into the mystery and magic of distance, until elves and fairies become possible to the imagination.

Roslin Castle was for centuries the residence of 'the lordly line of high St Clair', Barons of Roslin, Earls of Orkney and Caithness and later Dukes of Oldenburg, and a fortress must have existed here as early as 1100, when records show a William de St Clair in possession of the Barony of Roslin. The edifice whose ruins attract the visitor today was built by Sir William de St Clair, one of those noblemen who carried the heart of Robert the Bruce to Palestine. It consists of a central keep with adjoining buildings branching out from it. The family continued to increase in wealth and splendour until their glory culminated in the middle of the fifteenth century, when the magnificence of William, Earl of Orkney, and his wife Margaret, far surpassed that which had often sufficed for the Kings of Scotland. He was

Opposite:

ROSLIN CASTLE

38

served at his own table in vessels of gold and silver, borne by the lesser nobility; she was waited on by 75 gentlewomen, all clothed in velvet and silk and adorned with chains of gold. Badly damaged by fire in 1452, the castle was almost demolished during the English invasion of 1544, partially restored, then injured again in 1650 and has never been fully repaired.

Skirting round the east side of Edinburgh, one reaches Leith, the principal port. Leith was once much superior in population and status to its near neighbour, but in 1329 Robert the Bruce made a grant of the harbour and village to the town of Edinburgh. In 1398 Sir Robert Logan of Restalrig, a local landowner, contested the right of the Bruce to assign what was not his to give and compelled the citizens of Edinburgh to purchase a ratification from him.

Under this document there accrued to them the exclusive privilege of carrying on every species of traffic in the town, also of keeping inns and warehouses for the reception of travellers and the storing of their goods. In addition to this, in order to prevent the inhabitants of Leith from rivalling or competing with the citizens of Edinburgh in trade, the magistrates of the capital passed an act ordaining that:

> No merchant of Edinburgh should presume to take into partnership with him an inhabitant of Leith, under the penalty of 40 shillings Scots to the Church work, and to be deprived of the freedom of the town for one year; also that none of the town's revenues should be let to an inhabitant of Leith, nor any of the 'farmers' of the said revenues take a Leither as a partner in any contract relative to the same under the above penalties.

Leith remained officially subject to the 'superiority' of its larger neighbour from that date until 1832, when the provisions of the first great Reform Bill came into force.

A further few miles up the coast from Leith is the picturesque fishing village of Newhaven, with its pier and little harbour. The community here is, according to tradition, strictly exclusive. The fishing lads and lasses intermarry only among themselves, or with their kinsfolk of Fisherrow (Musselburgh). The women have their distinctive dress, wherein a multiplicity of gaily coloured petticoats is a prominent feature. Of considerable antiquity, dating back in fact to 1505, when James IV was building his mighty fishing vessel *The Great Michael*, many of the houses have carvings and inscriptions upon them which carry their erection back to the sixteenth and seventeenth centuries.

Further up the coast again lies Cramond – 'the fort on the Almond' – originally a Pictish or Gaelic fort, then a station for Roman legions; the great Roman road from the south passes close by. Cramond has always retained many historic and antiquarian associations. At the mouth of the river is the 'Cobble Ferry', by which the traveller crosses to the other side, a boon he owes to the former Prime Minister Lord Rosebery. The scenery here is surpassingly rich, the woods clothing the banks of the river down to the water's edge, while the village nestles amidst the greenery, a beautiful picture of rural peace and seclusion. About half a mile off the coat lie Cramond Isle and Inch Mickery, the latter little more than a bare rock.

Striking up the river bank for some little distance one may view the famous scene of 'The Twa Brigs'. The older bridge, dating back to the fifteenth century, consists of three pointed arches, the piers of which are strengthened by heavy buttresses. It has frequently been repaired, having become ruinous as early as 1607, but early in the nineteenth century, its stability being in doubt, a massive new bridge of eight arches was erected by the great engineer and bridge-builder John Rennie, whose work can also be seen in Kelso, Musselburgh and London, where he built the old Southwark and Waterloo Bridges and planned London Bridge.

The old bridge will always be remembered as the scene of the wooing of the

Twa Brigs

'Gudeman of Ballangeich', one of the numerous names and disguises of James V. According to tradition, the king had been flirting with a pretty country maiden, when he was discovered and assaulted by her father and brothers, along with her rustic suitor, and would have fared badly had not a labourer by the name of Jock Howieson, who was threshing grain with a flail at some little distance, observed the unequal contest. Asserting that in any contest of six against one, he would be on the side of the one, he threw himself into the combat, whirling his formidable flail. Speedily disabling his opponents, he saved the king from serious injury. The grateful monarch asked him to come to Holyrood and ask for the 'Gudeman of Ballangeich'. Howieson went, and was rewarded with the farm of Braehead, which his descendants held for over 300 years, on condition of presenting a ewer, basin and towel for the king to wash his hands when he passed the farm. This service was performed for George IV in 1822 and Queen Victoria in 1842.

Leaving the capital from the north, one cannot help but be struck by the magnificence of the Forth Railway Bridge. If one stands on the little pier at South Queensferry, this stupendous fabric, one of the greatest marvels of engineering of its day, towers overhead. It was completed and opened in 1890. Constructed on the cantilever or bracket system, which has been in use among the Chinese for over 2500 years, it consists of north and south approach viaducts, three huge double cantilevers of Siemen's rolled steel, whose brackets extend 680 feet north and south, with tubular towers exceeding St Paul's Cathedral in height. On a clear day the bridge is discernible from Edinburgh. The rail traveller might choose next to cross this bridge and penetrate into wilder and less populous parts of the country.

Opposite:

FORTH BRIDGE

THE HIGHLANDS

'Are there any countries, father, where no mountains are?' enquired the son of the Swiss hero William Tell, and when he was told that there were, his sympathies went out to the dwellers in the plains who were deprived of the natural grandeur with which he was surrounded. The level country may be exceedingly fair, its flower-spangled meadows may speak of peace and tranquillity, the murmur of its calm-flowing rivers may lull the senses into a pleasant languor, but these charms take little hold upon the mountain dweller whose heart is ever longing for the wild freedom of his native home.

The characteristics which stamp the individuality of a nation are the result, to a large extent, of the natural formation of the country; while the contrasts of mountain and valley, field and forest, loch and moorland, are reflected in those delicate traits of character which distinguish the dwellers in various portions of the same land. In all countries there is a strongly marked difference between the natives of the mountainous districts and those whose early days have been spent in the lowlands or plains. In no country is this contrast more noticeable than in Scotland, where the Highlanders and Lowlanders were kept apart for many centuries by a difference in language which proved a mightier barrier even than the Grampians. To the average 'southeron' of the past, the Highlands were a *terra incognita*, and he was considered a brave man in deed who would risk his life by penetrating the fastnesses of the North. Much of the danger and difficulty was purely imaginary, but none the less terrifying to the uneducated or untravelled.

MOOR NEAR KILLIN

47

The nature of the Highlander is highly poetical, for poetry has ever a fondness for mountainous districts, where she comes as a gentle comforter to soften the lot of the upland dwellers who have to endure weather discomforts unknown to the inhabitants of the plains. It has been said of Switzerland 'hard people, hard faith and very hard soil', and so it is with Scotland; and just as the mountain climate strengthens the saps and fibres of vegetation, so it will affect the mental and physical conditions of the people.

Although the weather conditions which prevail in the North during certain portions of the year may not prove attractive to the visitor, there is one season to which this does not apply, for nowhere is autumn more beautiful than in the Scottish Highlands, and the colour-effects produced by the sun, as it sinks behind some mighty ben, are gorgeous beyond description. The purple heather seems aflame, and even the grey rocks reflect its warm glow and stand out from their setting of green like giant amethysts from a bed of emeralds.

Should the enraptured stranger, while gazing upon the wondrous beauty and grandeur of the Highlands, hear at the same time the distant sounds of the bagpipes, the mental impression will be complete, and will remain as long as memory lasts. To one unaccustomed to the wild strains of the bagpipe, the sounds produced are at first bewildering and almost hateful, but gradually he comes under the spell and begins to understand what it means to the Highlander. His mind travels back into history, when the glens were peopled and the pibroch, the cry of the pipes, summoned the clans to battle. Should the visitor linger in the solitudes till the shades of night appear and the voice of Nature is lulled to sleep, then folklore and legend lift their heads and repeople the earth.

A Typical Perthshire Landscape

The tourist who visits the Highlands of Scotland will be amply repaid for his expenditure of time and money by what he sees, but he who can sojourn among the people will both see and hear what is hidden to the bird of passage. He will, in the remote parts, discover conditions of life of the most primitive description, and enter dwellings the architecture of which speaks of almost prehistoric times. He will find people contented to live as their forefathers lived, and to whom discomforts seem to appear as the natural conditions of everyday life. In studying the present in the lonely glens, he will be able to make the distant past live again, and the pages of history will be imbued with a living reality hitherto unknown to him. But he need not confine his investigations to the cottages of the poor, for the homes of the wealthy still retain enough of the old Highland dignity which marked the days when clan allegiance was unbroken, and the word of the chief was the only law known in the ranks of the clansmen.

So wrote an eloquent Scot in 1905, conjuring the beauties of his homeland. And indeed the country abounds with castles. Edinburgh has been mentioned, and inextricably linked with its history is that of Stirling, where the Scottish kings once held court, where the young James II was detained after being kidnapped by his own mother in her constant battle with her son's chancellor and regent; and where James V, Mary Queen of Scots and James VI were all crowned as infants.

There are castles at Aboyne and of course Balmoral on the Dee, and a fantastic Renaissance fairy-tale castle at Craigievar on the Don. One of the most spectacular of all is Dunnotter, on the Aberdeenshire coast near Stonehaven. This great fortress stands on a rock by the sea and can be reached only on foot. Here in 1645 the Duke of Montrose besieged the Earl Marischal of Scotland but failed to dislodge him; here too the Scottish Crown Jewels were hidden at the time of the English Civil War, when the Scots Privy Council feared lest they fall into the hands of Cromwell.

DUNOTTER CASTLE

Although history records that an ancestor of Lord Lovat lurked for six weeks in a secret chamber of Cawdor Castle after the Battle of Culloden, the name is most familiar to lovers of Shakespeare. It is being endowed with the title Thane of Cawdor that sets Macbeth on his ambitious and murderous course, for this fulfils the first part of the Weird Sisters' prophecy; they have also promised that he shall be 'king hereafter' and, according to the Bard, Macbeth and his wife prefer not to trust in Providence but take the matter into their own hands. Macbeth's own castle was probably much further south, on Dunsinnan hill, not far from Perth; the supposed site commands a fine prospect of the Grampians with Birnam Wood in the foreground. Shakespeare, and the legend he followed, take no account of the fact that a considerable river guarded Dunsinane, as he called it, from hostile advances from its distant neighbour. Yet some natives of these parts have convinced themselves that the author of *Macbeth* must have known the neighbourhood. One conjecture, recorded by a nineteenth-century chronicler, is that he visited Perth with a far-strolling troop of actors:

'You will say next that Shakespeare was Scotch!' exclaimed a scornful southerner to a Scot who seemed to take too patriotic a view of the matter.

'Weel,' came the cautious answer, 'his ability would warrant the supposeetion.'

As for Macbeth and his good lady, there have been serious attempts to whitewash their characters. No doubt these two worthies represented the good old Scottish party, set sternly against the Anglican influences introduced through Malcolm Canmore and his English wife, the Margaret who founded the

Opposite:

Cawdor Castle

52

chapel in Edinburgh Castle, in favour of whose family the English poet shows a natural bias. Did we know the whole truth, that same Duncan whom Shakespeare portrays as so meek and gracious may have had a scheme to serve the Macbeths as the Macdonalds of Glencoe were served by their guests the Campbells. The one thing clear in early Scottish history is that the dagger played a greater part than the ballot box, and that scandals in high life might sometimes be obscured by an eloquent advocate on one side or other. Sir Walter Scott suggests that Macbeth probably met Duncan in fair fight somewhere near Elgin; and the scene of his own defeat seems to have been the Mar country rather than the Tay valley.

Nor far from Elgin or Cawdor, Urquhart Castle is a ruin now, brooding over the dark waters of Loch Ness. Here talk of a monster dates back to the time of St Columba, whose boat is said to have been towed across the water by an unknown beast, to whom the saint then granted perpetual freedom of the loch.

The waters are dark because the loch is fed by eight rivers and innumerable streams which carry with them the peat from the mountains; but the darkness seems particularly apt here. The Falls of Foyers, which roar to the east of the loch, are another awesome feature:

Here is solitude with a vengeance – stern, grim, dungeon solitude! How ghostlike those white, skeleton pines, stripped of their rind by tempest and lightning, and dead to the din of the raging cauldron! That cataract, if descending on a cathedral, would shatter down the pile into a million of fragments. But it meets the black foundations of the cliff, and flies up to the starless heaven in a storm of spray. We are drenched, as if leaning in a hurricane over the gunwale of a ship, rolling under bare poles through a heavy sea. The very solid globe of earth quakes through her entrails. The eye, reconciled to the darkness, now sees a glimmering and a

gloomy light – and lo, a bridge of a single arch hung across the chasm, just high enough to let through the triumphant torrent. Has some hill-loch burst its barriers? For what a world of waters come now tumbling into the abyss! Niagara! hast thou a fiercer roar? Listen – and you think there are momentary pauses in the thunder, filled up with goblin groans! All the military music-bands of the army of Britain would here be dumb as mutes – Trumpet, Cymbal, and the Great Drum! There is a desperate temptation in the hubbub to leap into destruction. Water-horses and kelpies, keep stabled in your rock-stalls – for if you issue forth the river will sweep you down, before you have finished one neigh, to Castle Urquhart, and dash you, in a sheet of foam, to the top of her rocking battlements…

We emerge, like a gay creature of the elements, from the chasm, and wing our way up the glen towards the source of the cataract. In a few miles all is silent. A more peaceful place is not among all the mountains. The water-spout that had fallen during night has found its way into Loch Ness, and the torrent has subsided into a burn.

Loch Ness itself forms part of the Great Glen, a geological fault line that slashes across the northern part of Scotland, dividing what some would call the true Highlands from that rather less wild region which tourists have long since discovered. From either side of the cleft smaller glens and straths, each the 'country' of some clan, debouch into Glenmore, bed of a chain of lochs and streams linked together as the Caledonian Canal, their varying levels made navigable by the locks that come more easily to an English tongue. In the century before the canal's trenches were opened, King George's soldiers had isolated the farther Highlands by means of a road between three fortified posts, in the centre and at either end of the Great Glen, which were used as a base for dominating and 'civilising' a region over which the fiery cross ran more freely than the King's writ.

RIVER AWE, ARGYLSHIRE

Inverness is called the capital of the Highlands, though it lies on the edge of Celtic Scotland, at the north end of the Great Glen and near the head of the Moray Firth. It is not a Gaelic city – its inhabitants had at one time the reputation of speaking the best English in Scotland, or, for the matter of that, in England, a quality sometimes traced back to a colony of Cromwell's soldiers. This had changed by the turn of the last century:

> Although the speech of the town no longer merits this accolade, yet still in some of the secluded glens of the county may be heard a tongue not their own used with a melodious refinement unknown within the sound of Bow Bells.

Loch Oich, the much smaller loch linked to Loch Ness by the Caledonian Canal, has an authentic legend as the retreat of Ewen Macphee, perhaps the last British outlaw above the rank of a lurking poacher or illicit distiller. Early in the nineteenth century he enlisted in a Highland regiment, from which he deserted and, although captured and handcuffed, made a romantic escape to his native wilds of Glengarry:

> After camping in the woods till the hue and cry after him had died out, he settled on an islet of Loch Oich, where he took a wife and reared a sturdy brood of children. For a long time he played Rob Roy on a small scale, 'lifting' sheep and helping himself to game, while enjoying the sanctity of a seer's reputation. When a southern landlord bought the property he established a not unfriendly way of living with this unofficial tenant, who introduced himself to the new owner by sticking his dagger into the table as title-deed to his island: 'By this right I hold it!'

> But by and by the minions of the law pressed upon his retreat; and in spite of a resolute defence he was arrested for sheep stealing and taken to prison, where he pined away after a long life of lawless freedom. Bales of sheep skins and tallow, found hidden about his

abandoned home, were evidence of how he had lived at the expense of his neighbours, a feature too much left out of sight in modern regret for the picturesque old times.

If the pensive tourist seeks a pure vision of the past, let him go out to the lonely station of Culloden Moor, some half a dozen miles from Inverness. Crossing the river Nairn and mounting the heights that will lead him over Drumossie, where 'the romantic cause of the Jacobites fell hopelessly when Cumberland's redcoats mowed down and bayoneted its weary champions', more than a tenth of whom died here for the forlorn sake of Bonnie Prince Charlie. Much has been written in praise of these gallant Highlanders:

> Fir plantations and fields now cover the wild nakedness of this tableland; but by the roadside are seen the mounds beneath which lie each clan together, still shoulder to shoulder, and the monumental cairn that is yearly hung with votive wreaths by certain fervent Jacobites. If these men gave way before the disciplined valour and artillery of the English, if their own martial spirit was marred by quarrelsome ill-temper, let us remember how many of them joined or rejoined the cause when it was as good as lost, after the Jacobite squires of the south had held back from its first flush of success.

> Let us consider how neither bribes, nor threats, nor torture could tempt these poor Highlanders to betray their prince in his desperate wanderings, despite the price set on his head. One poor fellow took hundreds of lashes on an English ship of war, without opening his mouth to confess that he had ferried the fugitive to a safer island.

The visitor who ventures north of Inverness has probably set his sights on John o' Groats, but there are one or two places on the way that might give him reason to pause. Dingwall, the little county town of Ross, has been

CROFT NEAR DALMALLY

fondly thought to resemble Jerusalem in site. Strathpeffer, the 'Scottish Harrogate' began to thrive when it got a railway. A contemporary account records that...

> ...till then its clients were chiefly local, many of them seeking an antidote to more potent waters distilled hereabouts; but the advent of trains brought visitors from both sides of the border. Strathpeffer has varied advantages to bring visitors all the way from London, notably the strongest sulphur water in the kingdom and an effervescing mineral spring on a kind more commonly found in Germany than in Britain.

In Wester Ross lies Loch Maree, which some judge the finest scene in Scotland. Less smiling than Loch Lomond, it lies more wildly among naked pyramids of quartz, Ben Slioch the most conspicuous point of them, but this lake has the same beauty of wooded islets at the lower end, where a group of half-drowned hillocks form a miniature archipelago, grey with lichened stone and wooded with birch and hazel. On one of these are the ruin of a chapel of the Virgin Mary, after whom Loch Maree may be named. Beyond it open the sea-inlets Torridon, Gairloch and Loch Ewe; and the coast northwards by Ullapool and Loch Inver is pierced by deep fiords and overlooked by grand summits, worn down from Himalayan masses of old.

Among all the clans who once ruled the Highlands, the most numerous and the most powerful in recent history have been the Campbells, who rose on the wreck on the once predominant Macdonalds, ousting and absorbing men of other less auspicious names till the new lords were firmly seated over Argyll and a large part of Perthshire. They owed this prosperity to a knack of choosing the stronger side, whereas Highlanders (as at Culloden)have been more apt to figure as champions of falling causes. While less practically minded stocks stood 'agin the government', the Campbells usually proved ready to recognise *de facto* authority, to catch the flowing tide of fortune and to turn even godliness to gain.

TYPICAL ROSS SCENERY

The worst thing that has been said about the Campbells is that they played police for the throne – what the Jacobites perceived as the unlawful, English throne – for profit, and were too ready to root out their own turbulent enemies in the name of law. The story of the Glencoe massacre is renowned among many such deeds of cruelty which have stained the heather, but it is not always recognised to what extent this was a slaughter of Macdonalds by their hereditary enemies the Campbells, acting under legal authority.

The legendary Gaelic poet Ossian is said to have been born in Glencoe, and there could be no more fitting birthplace. It has been written that its serrated and bristling walls 'have a barren strength and steepness which remind one continually of the stone buttresses of Sinai'; yet the sunlight shows weird Arabesque colourings of purple, green and pink, often dulled beneath a pall that seems nature's mourning for the tragedy here commemorated by a cross, and its scene still traced out by patches of green round the site of ruined huts. 'Even with sunshine,' the poet and historian Macaulay found this 'the very valley of the shadow of death'.

Glencoe, Ben Cruachan and other outskirts of this area rank among the wildest scenes in Scotland. Loch Awe and Loch Etive are hardly surpassed in fame. The general aspect of this region, however, seems a blending of true Highland and semi-Lowland, like the character and career of its lords. The writer Robert Buchanan tells us how it is...

> ...fair and gentle, a green pastoral land, where the sheep bleat from a thousand hills, and the grey homestead stands in the midst of its own green fields, and the snug macadamised roads ramify in all directions from the tiny capital on the seaside, with the country carts bearing produce, the drouthy [thirsty] farmer trotting home at all hours on his sure-footed nag, and the stage coach, swift and gay, wakening up the echoes in summer time with the guard's cheery hurn.

Even its wilder nooks, as one can see from coach, railway or steamer, have been much broken up as sites for mansions and villas, hotels and shooting-lodges; and in summer months farms and cottages in a hundred glens are packed tight with holiday-making families from the cities, whose seaside retreats threaten to turn the arms of the Clyde into a gigantic Venice.

The tiny capital to which Buchanan refers is Inverary, a big village picturesquely situated on a sea loch under the shade of lordly woods about the duke's castle, which in the early years of the twentieth century first underwent the indignity of being let to a Southerner.

But tamed and trimmed as much of this 'Campbell country' has been, no Highland region shows more variously those aspects of earth and sky, sublime, stern, sad and sometimes tender, that seem reflected in the character of the people. The great Scottish geologist Sir Archibald Geikie, who pushes scientific candour to the point of hinting that the Battle of Bannockburn would have gone otherwise had the ground been drained, finds the Highlander's nature moulded by his rugged hills and streaming glens. The contrast between the Scottish and the Irish Gael, which some would explain by the former's stronger strain of Norse blood, this author accounts for rather by the fact of the latter enjoying a milder climate, a better soil and more level fields, that give fairer play to the natural buoyancy, good-humour and quick wit of the Celt.

> In the Highlander, on the other hand, these characteristics have been replaced by a reserved, self-restrained, even somewhat sullen and morose disposition. He is neither merry nor witty like his cousin across the Irish Channel. Yet he is courteous, dutiful, persevering, a courageous foe, an unwavering ally. I am disposed

Opposite:

INVERARY CROSS AND CASTLE

to regard this difference in temperament as traceable in great measure to the peculiar condition of the Highlander's environment. Placed in a glen, often narrow and rocky, and separated from his neighbours in the next glens by high ranges of rugged hills, he has had to contend with a scant and stony soil, and a wet, cold and uncertain climate. He has to wage with the elements a never-ending battle, wherein he is often the loser. He stands among the mountains face to face with nature in her wilder moods. Storm and tempest, mist-wreath and whirlwind, the roar of waterfalls, the rush of swollen streams, the crash of loosened landslips, which he may seem hardly to notice, do not pass without bringing, unconsciously perhaps, to his imagination their ministry of terror. Hence the playful mirthfulness and the light-hearted ease of the Celtic temperament have, in his case, been curdled into a stubbornness which may be stolid obstinacy or undaunted perseverance, according to the circumstances which develop it. Like his own granite hills, he has grown hard and enduring, not without a tinge of melancholy, suggestive of the sadness that lingers among his wind-swept glens, and that hangs about the bracken slops around his lonely lakes.

Another observer continues the theme of the effect of the land on the Scottish character:

There is little need to point out the stronger contrast between this dweller beside hungry mountains or cruel seas, and the otherwise mingled race that has grown stout, ruddy and jovial on Lowland or Midland plains, among green pastures and still waters, where the cattle, hardly raising a head to look beyond their own hedgerows, may well be content with their lot, and the very dogs, familiar and placable, will not always trouble to wag a tail at the wayfarer. Generations of ancient peace have here tamed men's spirits, quieted their fears, and worn down their reverence to a

sober respect for honesty, good-fellowship, good-nature, prudence, prosperity, all the qualities which make neighbours pleasant company. A charm of homeliness rests upon churches, halls, farms and hamlets, scattered roomily in secure confidence, where man may well nestle in the kindly lap of earth and rejoice in nature's gifts to a generation for which rough edges of peril have been blunted by use and wont.

But if nature has shaped the lives and character of the Scottish mainlander, how much more effect has she had on the inhabitants of the distant and windswept isles.

Opposite:

THE WAIT

THE ORKNEYS AND SHETLANDS

The Orkney and Shetland Isles, whoever were their original inhabitants, became restocked from the kingdom that figures in legendary history as 'Lochlin', and still plainly keep much of the Scandinavian character, which on other coasts of Britain appears only in patches and strains or, as in the Southern Hebrides, overlaid by Celtic features. These northern islands had early been known to Gothic pirates, crushing the early Christianity believed to have been planted by disciples of St Columba from his base on Iona. The Norwegian kingdom, converted to Christianity in its turn, established its power more or less firmly all over the Hebrides, with occasional assaults on Ireland and Scotland; and for three centuries the Orkneys were a 'Jarldom' dependent on Norway. The Icelandic sagas throw a weird light on their confused history of feuds, treacheries, fire and sword, bouts of drinking and devotion, from which, as the Kingdom of Scotland took shape, began to emerge a rivalry between the claims of kinship and those of proximity.

In short, when the last Norwegian invasion was defeated on the Clyde in 1263, all the outer islands were formally returned from Norway to Scotland, with the exception of Orkney and Shetland, which were specially reserved to the Norwegian crown (later itself absorbed into that of Denmark). But two centuries later, when differences between the thrones of Denmark and Scotland came to be adjusted by the marriage of King James III to Margaret of Denmark, her father pledged the islands to Scotland as a guarantee against the bulk of her stipulated dowry, 60,000 florins, which were never paid. So Scotland owns this part of her realm in the capacity of a pawnbroker's, as to which international lawyers might cover acres of paper, should Denmark be disposed to pay off the mortgage.

ORCADEAN FIREPLACE

73

Even earlier, Sinclairs and other lords from the mainland had pushed on to the Orkneys, which afterwards became so oppressively exploited by the hungry Scots that theirs was no beloved name there; and many of the islanders, even now that old resentments are forgotten, decline to look on themselves as Scotsmen.

Except by isolated incidents, the islands have entered little into the history of Scotland, since the days when it was alternately a refuge and a raiding ground for their Viking chiefs. Kirkcaldy of Grange – one of the early Protestants who murdered Cardianl Beaton (see page 24) – was shipwrecked here in pursuit of Bothwell in 1567. In the seventeenth century General Montrose pressed some of the islanders into his service; otherwise they took slight interest in the wars of Whig and Tory which occupied the attention of so much of the rest of the country. More than one stirring naval engagement took place at this northern end of the kingdom, long exposed to raids from French and Dutch cruisers, against which, indeed, most of the islands were well defended by their perilous reefs and currents. Much later the Shetlands were in the news again when a hoax deceived newspaper readers of 1866 into believing the account of a Fenian raid on the northernmost island of Unst, with such details as a forced ransom, the taking of hostages, the minister hanged by his own bell-rope, all set forth so seriously that a man-of-war is said to have got as far as Aberdeen on its way to the rescue.

The two groups number some 160 islands and islets, fewer than half of them inhabited. Lying in the Gulf Stream, they have a wet and windy climate, variable rather than severe, often cool in summer, raw and rheumatic in winter, when a truly dark December affords little chance for skating or curling. That many-weathered March of the British Isles usually brings the sharpest cold to this end of them. The whole archipelago is so broken into

Opposite:

THE LACEMAKER

holms (islets) and indented by voes (bays) that on the largest islands one will never be more than a few miles from the sea; nor is it easy to take a mile's walk without coming on a reed-fringed, foam-edged basin of fresh water, over which salt spray blows into one's face across the rough, cliff-bound flats that swell up into waves of moor, but seldom into imposing hills. Except in a few favoured spots, where thin clumps of stunted wood are nursed like gardens, a telegraph post is the only kind of tree breaking the bleak horizon above heath and bog, with a lonely farmhouse, a huddle of cottages, a patch of fields now and then to remind one that this is no wilderness.

Seen under its too frequent shade of sullen sky or drizzling showers, such a landscape strikes the lover of lush nature as dismal, yet it has its bright moments, sometimes its halcyon seasons in the long days of the far northern summers, and at all times taking features of its own. One guide to the islands describes it thus:

> The scene, which on a sunless day seems hard and cold, with occasional gleams of sunlight becomes a perfect kaleidoscope of varying colours.

That writer goes on to describe the vivid greens of early summer, the glorious shows of red clover that relieve the prevalent dullness, and the rich spangling of spring flowerets that here linger into June and July.

Another writer sums up the islands' finest features like this:

> For the artists there are vast spaces of sea and sky; the shining sands; the glories of the sunset; and above and beyond all the pageantry of the storm. For each day a fresh drama is transacted upon the heavens. The morning hours are often brilliantly bright; but ere mid-day the sun is suddenly obscured; the storm-cloud rises out of the Atlantic; sometimes the wind and rain lash the panes for hours; sometimes the cloud breaks upon the hills of Hoy

and passes away like a dream. The *dénouement* of the drama is always obscure; you cannot predict what the end will be, and so the interest never flags. And among the land-locked bays and through the narrow channels there is excellent boating for those who can circumvent the tides. Unless, indeed, you know something of the obscure laws which govern the ebb and flow of the ocean in this network of islands, you are pretty sure to come to grief. For round many of them it runs like a mill-race…But if you study the tides, you can seek out secluded nooks, where the seals are basking on the tangle, and the wild duck are wheeling round the bay, and the blue rocks are darting out of the caves, and the grouse are crowing among the heather, and where for ten months out of the twelve the peace is absolute, and silence unbroken save for the shepherd's dog.

It has been remarked how the very superstitions of such a land run to fishiness, as indeed all over these islands uncouth leviathans haunt the fog banks, dragons lurk in the hollowed cliffs, sea-serpents in the voes as water-bulls in the lochans, and treacherously smiling mermaids, more to be shunned than all these monsters, delude men to their doom among slippery reefs. The mermaid legends may well have been suggested by half-human glimpses of seals. Our critical age is also disposed to relate them to occasional visits of Eskimo or Lapp adventurers, seen only to the waist in their skin canoes. Not so long ago there were people in the islands who boasted descent from 'Finn' strangers, very possibly kinsmen of an aboriginal pigmy race, Picts, 'Pechts' or what not, that may here have left their memory in the 'Trows' or 'Trolls' of land mythology, and their name in the Pentland (Pechtland) Firth.

The ground was once much divided among small proprietors – as it still is to

opposite:

REDDIN' THE LINE

a lesser degree – and small-holdings are common. The Orcadians had their fit of standing out obstinately against 'improvements'; then they suffered from the set-back of the kelp industry, here very profitable for a time, but its failure proved a blessing in disguise, as it forced them to turn their attention to agriculture; and they seem too well off now to trouble about kelp. Towards the end of the nineteenth century there grew up a flourishing export of cattle, much improved by the introduction of good stock. Along with their ponies and hairy sheep, almost as wild as goats, the islands had a breed of small cows, from whose milk was made their peculiar buttermilk drink *bland*. An effort was once made to push this beverage in London, where it seems not to have 'caught on'. A Scottish writer then living in lodgings in London recorded that he patriotically ordered a case of it…

> …which, as the weather was hot and the liquor 'up', I put under my bed, taking this for the coolest spot at my command, but ignorant that it was over the kitchen fire. I had hardly got into bed when, one by one, the bottles began to explode, till the whole battery had fired itself away. Above me slept no less a fellow-lodger than General Gordon, not yet of Khartoum; and I wondered whether my bombardment might have brought China into his dreams.

The Shetlands, for their part, are grander, wilder, rougher, poorer, colder, wetter, less 'improved' – in general more Norse and primitive. Their industry is rather at sea than on land. An apt saying as to the difference between the people claims that 'the Shetlander is a fisherman who has a farm; the Orcadian a farmer who has a boat'.

Through the fisheries the Shetlanders were long in closer touch with Holland and Scandinavia than with Scotland, which for centuries had been spreading her tentacles over the adjacent Orkneys. In the reign of George III (1760–1820) Dutch and Danish coins were more familiar to Lerwick than the head of their own monarch; and up to a later time Norwegian weights

and measures were used all over the islands. The Orkneys are, or were, well stocked with grouse and snipe; sea-fowl are the game of the Shetlands, not that they are lacking in the southern group. The Orkneys are rich in cattle, the Shetlands rather in sheep, where the chief home industry is the hosiery knitting that keeps women's fingers busy even when their backs are bowed under peat creels. The Shetlands, in short, bear much the same relation to the Orkneys as the Highlands to the Lowlands. Till lately the Shetlands were less visited by strangers; but now a tide of tourist travel seems to be setting strongly to the northern isles, which offer such a change of air for southerners able to put up with somewhat basic accommodation, while hospitable good-will as yet must take the place of hotel luxury.

Opposite:

SKYE CROFTER

THE HEBRIDES

Old books speak of the Western Islands as sacred, some of the smallest among them appearing specially hallowed ground. How did successive adorations come to be concentrated on the low, bare islet of Iona, lying a mile off the farther point of that long promontory called the Ross of Mull? From the dawn of legend it seems to wear a misty halo. Its oldest name mean '*the* island'; in Gaelic it is the Isle of the Druids; then its alternative name of *Icolmkill* embalms the memory of St Columba, who from this beacon-fire lit the Gospel all over the Highlands.

Palladius is said to have been the earliest missionary to Scotland. He was closely followed by St Ninian, whose light seems to have smouldered on the savage shores of Galloway, till from his dying hand St Patrick in the fifth century carried it over to Ireland to blaze up before half of Europe. From this school of piety and learning in the next century came St Columba, as penance for sin devoting himself to the conversion of the wild Picts. The legend goes that he first disembarked on Oronsay, but quitted it because thence he could still catch sight of his beloved Ireland. Landing on Iona he buried his boat lest he should be tempted to return. But he had no sooner settled his little band in rough wattled buildings than they were building other coracle craft of wicker-work covered by skins, in which to launch forth on the perilous Hebridean seas and up the long inlet of lake and glen that opens up the heart of the Highlands. In the second half of his busy life Columba pushed repeated journeys to the far north, to the Orkneys, even, it is said, as far as Iceland, preaching through interpreters, founding mission stations and planting civilisation as well as faith among barbarous people.

Opposite:

IONA

With the double text of work and prayer, he taught his followers to make the best of that poor soil of Iona, from which such pregnant seeds went forth on every wind. He is said to have copied the gospel 300 times with his own hand. A nineteenth-century writer describes him thus:

> This saint had his weaknesses, those of his creed and time. He would allow no woman on Iona, nor even a cow, for 'where there is a cow, there is a woman; and where there is a woman…' – we know what monks thought of Eve's daughters. An adjacent islet was given up to a nest of nuns who had fluttered towards this cold halo. So great waxed the fame of Columba's sanctity that pilgrims sought his retreat from all parts of western Christendom; and a sore pilgrimage it must have been that ended at the point of Mull, where a miraculously strengthened hail would bring over a boat from the island. Still the saint's memory looms through a cloud of miracle and fable, behind which we catch the human proportions and qualities of a good strong man who had such power of winning hearts.

The Culdees, whom Presbyterians have claimed as spiritual forefathers, free from Popish error, are taken by many to be disciples of St Columba. But while Scotland went on being dotted with Culdee chapels and monasteries, Iona became a Christian Mecca as well as a centre of education and missions. The bodies of princes and chiefs were brought here to be buried in sacred ground. Sixty kings of Scotland, Ireland and Norway have been counted as buried in this little isle, some of them perhaps since before Columba's time. Duncan and Macbeth are fabled to lie here side by side; yet when the list reaches more authentic kings, this royal sepulchre seems no longer to have been so revered, for even Alexander II, who in 1249 died conveniently close

opposite:

SKYE SPINNING

on the island of Kerrera, was carried for burial all the way to Melrose.

There can be no more impressive sight than the burial-ground with its sculptured stones and worn crosses that now mark the undistinguished dust of men who at least 'did not expect to be so soon forgotten'. By the twelfth century Cluniac monks had taken the place of the original garrison, more than once broken up by raids of Norse pirates. The oldest building is St Oran's chapel, believed to have been erected by the same pious Queen Margaret who built the chapel in Edinburgh Castle. The Nunnery appears to be later work, and the cathedral to date from the thirteenth to the sixteenth century. These memorials, hastily visited by drenched and seasick tourists, make but fragments of the ecclesiastical state that once flourished on Iona. Its monuments were rudely treated at the Reformation, when all but two of 360 crosses may have been thrown into the sea by an iconoclastic Presbytery.

Skye has as many memories of Columba as if it had been the home of the saint whose name has been associated with more Western Highland chapels and caves than there are modern churches in this wide diocese of his. Near Iona, Colonsay is named after him, as Oronsay is named after his companion Oran, the ruins of a monastery still visible on the latter, and the abbey on the former not yet forgotten. But one cannot enumerate all the remains of ancient piety scattered over the Hebrides, in most cases ill accessible to hasty curiosity. The chances of reaching and in rough weather landing on those islands give one pause to consider how cut off from the world they were before the days of Watt and Macadam, and under what difficulties the sturdy apostles carried on their work.

What travel among those broken shores was before steamboats – the boarding of which from pierless islands may still be adventurous – can be guessed from David Balfour's troubled wanderings in Robert Louis Stevenson's *Kidnapped*, from the delays of Dr Johnson's difficult tour, faithfully recorded by his companion Boswell in *Journal of the Tour of the Hebrides,* and from the fact that when the Reverend Dr Norman Macleod

went to college in Glasgow in the 1830s, the journey from Morvern – not much over 80 miles as the crow flies –by land and water took ten days.

Nor has this stretch of the southern Hebrides much to tempt the general tourist from his lines of more luxurious travel. Some points well deserve an hotel and guide-book notice, such as the grand quartzite masses of the Paps of Jura, commanding a view from Skye to the Isle of Man; and the map of islets and inlets spread out, weather permitting, below Ben More of Mull, whose little white capital Tobermory has been compared to a damp Naples in respect of looking its best from the sea. One optimistic commentator proclaimed Mull 'the most beautiful of the western isles', but this is not a generally held view. Its coast makes a fretwork of rocky patterns that become monotonous, repeated in miniature upon some of the adjacent islets and peninsulas. But striking scenes may be too widely scattered among what at first sight seem featureless stretches of sea, moor and rock, that will not take every stranger's fancy in their common setting of mist and rain, out of which hasty comers and goers at Oban often carry away the impression of nothing more cheerful than its red-funnelled arks of escape from a hopeless deluge.

Yet these Highland coasts, dull or forbidding as they may look from the sea, warm into charmingness under loyal eyes like Norman Macleod's, that can never forget the wild play-place of a happy boyhood:

> A castled promontory, a range of dark precipices supporting the upland pastures, and streaked with white waterfalls, which are lost in the copse at their base, form a picture not very imposing compared with 'what one sees everywhere'. A long ridge of hill rising some two thousand feet above the sea, its brown sides, up to a certain height, chequered with green stripes and patches of

Opposite:

Tobermory

cultivation; brown heather-thatched cottages, with white walls; here and there a mansion, whose chimneys are seen above the trees which shelter it – these are the chief features along its seaboard of many miles. But how different is the whole scene when one lands! New beauties reveal themselves, and every object seems to change its size, appearance, and relative position. A rocky wall of wondrous beauty, the rampart of the old upraised beach which girdles Scotland, runs along the shore; the natural wild wood of ash, oak and birch, with the hazel copse, clothes the lower hills and shelters the herds of wandering cattle; lonely sequestered bays are everywhere scooped out into beautiful harbours; points and promontories seem to grow out of the land, and huge dykes of whinstone fashion to themselves the most picturesque outlines; clear streams everywhere hasten on to the sea; small glens, perfect gems of beauty, open up entrances into deep dark pools, hemmed in by steep banks hanging with ivy, honeysuckle, rowan-trees and ferns; while on the hillsides scattered cottages, small farms and shepherds' huts, the signs of culture and industry, give life to the whole scene.

Perhaps few people can really love West Highland scenery unless they have in youth grown familiar with every blush of heather, every skin of copse or bracken, every brown rib bared amid the turf, and all the moods of those stern features under changing lights and shadows. One surpassing glory of this region is the evening skies that may reward patient sufferers under rain. Walter Paton's Highland skyscapes were accused of being too Turneresque in their gorgeous hues; but they make no exaggeration of what a Gaelic bard calls 'the tartan of the sky'. The more lovely for their uncertainty are the day-long or week-long spells of fine weather that may come in the heart of a stormy summer, sometimes lasting a month or two while the plains of the south seem to draw away the freakish mountain clouds. Then in late autumn the west has often a truce of halcyon days brooding peacefully over horizons where Italian blue, touched with native softness, melts into a glassy sea among

the opening of richly tinted hills. And at all times the clearing after rain may produce effects which a city poet aptly compares to the raising of the curtain on a pantomime transformation scene. But as another writer puts it…

> …more often the face of this region shows overcast, in too true keeping with its gloomy traditions. The Christianity spread among these islanders seems long to have been but skin deep, where every ruin is haunted by memories of cruelty and hatred from days when the cross itself was dearest as a fiery summons to bloodshed. Between Lismore and Mull rises the Lady's Rock, on which Maclean of Duart let his wife, Argyll's daughter, be exposed to the mercy of the tide, by one account for no worse crime than that of being a Campbell; but a more elaborately romantic version brings in jealousy of a Spanish *señora* which urged this lady to procure the historical blowing up of an Armada ship. The lady's peril had a dramatic ending which made this an oft-told tale: she was rescued by fishermen of her father's clan, and when the husband came to Inverary clad in hypocritical woe, what seemed to him to be her ghost confronted him at the funeral feast that proved to be his own.

Skye is now the 'show island' of the west coast, easily invaded by its ferries, but comparatively few tourists trust themselves across the stormy Minches, Great and Little, to visit the Long Island, more foreign to thriving Scotland than Jersey is to England. One used to be told that the Minch was *La Manche*, the Highland Channel, as the *Kyles* so frequent here are called cousins with the straits of Calais; but a pundit of the Oxford Dictionary shakes his head at these as at most popular interpretations of place-names. The 120-mile chain of islands making a breakwater for north-western Scotland, with the Sunday name of the Outer Hebrides, is commonly spoken of as the Long Island, that once indeed formed one stretch of land, and still at some parts is cut only by fords passable at low tide.

The name Long Island should perhaps be restricted to the northern mass of Lewis and Harris, below which, across the Sound of Harris, the smaller separate isles taper out southwards like the tail of a kite, tipped by the lighthouse on Bernera shining 30 miles across the Atlantic.

It is no wonder if tourists do not often get so far, when till the last years of the nineteenth century the law had to make a long arm to reach the Hebrides, and the Protestant Reformation was only beginning to set foot on some of those remote strongholds of old ways and thoughts. Nine tourists out of ten, indeed, would find little to repay them for the tossing of the Minch. The archaeologist may wander his difficult way among monuments of the past, standing stones, 'Picts' houses', crosses and shrines whose site is often marked by no more than a gathering of lonely graves, for even of the chapels and hermitages recorded in print only a small proportion can now be traced in the Western Islands. The rich stranger encloses these islands for his deer, narrowing and debasing the already poor life of the people. Here and there snug inns invite anglers to sport such as Izaak Walton never dreamt of. Some parts show oases of real Highland scenery. But more often the Outer Hebrides present a bleak and monotonous aspect of rock, water, sand and bog, where 'the sea is all islands and the land is all lakes'. Their common features on half the days of the week are thus described by Robert Buchanan, who has been described as 'no bookworm to be afraid of a wet jacket'.

> A dreary sky, a dreary fall of rain. Long low flats covered with their own damp breath, through which the miserable cattle loomed like shadows. Everywhere lakes and pools, as thickly sown among the land as islands amid the Pacific waters.

The Long Island has more cheerful prospects in its blinks of sunshine, but there is hardly a tree, and every drifting log or plank of shipwreck washed up from the Atlantic is treasured to make the rafters of a human habitation. The wild carrot is the finest fruit that grows here naturally among the scent of the heather.

The islanders love their homes passionately, but they owe little to a thankless soil. The bulk of them are half croft-farmers, half fishers, the petty agricultural labours falling chiefly to the women's share, while the men alternate between spells of nautical adventure and lazy weather-watching. The wives and daughters have the worst of it, who in their daily tasks soon grow haggard, their eyes bleared by the smoke of the beehive huts in which they literally gather round the fire, amid furniture and utensils that often would not seem fit for a gypsy camp. In these hovels, hardly to be distinguished from the peat-stacks that shelter them, may still be found many time-honoured implements, and in some parts rough home-made pottery is but slowly displaced.

The trade of the islands is fishing, to which most of them are bound from boyhood, many wandering into far seas like their Viking forefathers; and the girls, too, make long excursions to serve as fish gutters and curers for the season in eastern ports, even as far as Yarmouth in Norfolk. Ling, cod and lobsters yield a valuable harvest; mussels and cockles are sent to metropolitan markets as relishes. Bonnie Prince Charlie's first meal on Scottish ground was off such vulgar shellfish, but he was to fare worse before all was done.

The chief game of their seas is, of course, the herring, which appears off the Hebridean coasts early in the season; and there may be an aftermath in autumn, the more enterprising fishers in summer following the shoals round to the east coast. Even on the warmer west coast the men armour themselves in such thick clothing that once overboard they would have little chance of escaping the clutches of Davy Jones, even had they learned to swim, an art not much cultivated in the Hebrides.

To youngsters a night in a fishing boat makes a pleasing taste of adventure,

Opposite:

At The Spinning Wheel

if the waves leave them appetite for coffee sweetened by treacle, and mackerel caught and cooked on board to be eaten with the hard biscuits that serve also for plates. Then it is a fine sight in the chill dawn, when the phosphorescent glow of floats and cordage pales before the sheen of the fish hauled up in wave after wave of silver; and one can catch the melancholy cheep of herrings as they flop out of the meshes of the net to swell a glittering pile among which the men move like mermaids, their legs and arms encrusted with scales. The geologist John MacCulloch noted the phosphorescence of summer nights in these seas, offering splendid phenomena to eyes more often keen for their profits than for their wonders:

> A stream of fire ran off on each side from the bows, and the ripple of the wake was spangled with the glow-worms of the deep. Every oar dropped diamonds, every fishing line was a line of light, the iron cable went down a torrent of flame, and the plunge of the anchor resembled an explosion of lightning. When it blew a gale the appearance was sometimes terrific, and the whole atmosphere was illuminated, as if the moon had been at the full. In calms, nothing could exceed the loveliness of the night, thus enlightened by thousands of lamps, which, as they sailed slowly by, twinkled and were again extinguished at intervals, on the glassy and silent surface of the water.

Early summer is the busy time of the Long Island, when Stornoway, Loch Boisdale, the Castle Bay of Barra and other havens make rendezvous for hundreds of boats of various rigs, and the population is increased by dealers from foreign shores, with many thousands of fish curers and gutters who, encamped in huts and bothies, are the followers of this fleet, attended also by mobs of greedy sea-gulls. The cream of the herring fishing goes to trawlers and other well-found craft from richer shores of our islands. The fish-curing business, too, like everything that needs capital, is much in the hands of strangers, the export being largely to the Baltic. The Hebridean boatmen live from hand to mouth, setting draughts of luck against blank days and weeks for which their competitors are better provided.

The Long Island proper is commonly conceived as two islands – Harris and Lewis – but the smaller southern projection is joined on to the main mass by a narrow isthmus. Nature has also set another distinction, the south part being boldly and barely mountainous, a forest of granite and gneiss peaks, amid which shy deer enjoy the beauties of this Hebridean Switzerland, while the north rather shows brown flats of moorland, rimmed with cliffs, streaked with green, dotted with patches of struggling culture and pitted with tiny lochs. All round, the shores are deeply cut with fiords. John Sinclair is one writer who has an artistic good word to say for Lewis:

> The shores are everywhere rugged and rocky, save where, at wide intervals, they are interrupted by broad bays or narrow sea lochs, which terminate in green glens among the hills. The middle and northern districts are for the most part great stretches of flat or undulating moorland, dotted all over with hundreds of little lochs and tarns, into which no burns tumble and out of which no rivers flow. Yet how pretty these flat saucers of rain-water are – scores and scores of them glistening in the sunshine like silver ornaments laid out to view upon a russet ground. In the south and south-west the mountains are thickly studded and lofty, but long twisting arms of the sea boldly creep in between them and almost meet from opposite sides of the island. Many of these inlets taper away to narrow points, which are hidden in deep valleys eight or ten miles from the open sea. So many are the fresh-water lochs and the insinuating arms of the ocean, that in bird's-eye view the whole island must resemble a diamond window with its countless raindrops darting one into another at the beginning of a shower. The hill tops are singularly wild and bare, scarcely a tinge of green relieving the yellow masses of rock and stone, but in the valleys there are many choice spots of sweet verdure and beauty.

On the neck of an eastern peninsula of Lewis stands Stornoway, which to the islanders appears a capital of dazzling luxury, and even strangers are struck

by the gardens nursed into exotic luxuriance about its castle. On the west side of the island stands the most celebrated and the least destructible of ancient monuments, the Stones of Callernish, which used to pass for a Druid temple, when there was as much reason for entitling them a Druid theatre, town-hall or house of parliament, if not the tomb of some once towering hero long gone to Valhalla. The figure of a cross has been traced in their position, on which account they have been credited to St Columba, the truth being that their origin is as mysterious as that of Stonehenge.

GLASGOW AND THE CLYDE

Modern writers have often been unkind about Glasgow, but all the early travellers extolled the prettiness, pleasantness and cleanness of this city on a once limpid river, qualities that have not always been apparent. Along with its share of squalid slums, Glasgow has fine features in her ancient cathedral, her lofty necropolis, her picturesque Trongate, her noble university buildings elevated about the West End Park. But none of these monuments is as remarkable as the wealth and manifold industry of which signs abound on every hand. Her rise to prominence has been described thus:

> In the middle of the eighteenth century, Glasgow had fewer than 20,000 inhabitants, but she began to make her fortune fast while the rest of Scotland rather sullenly prepared to exchange thistly patriotism for more profitable crops. Rum and tobacco were the foundation of a prosperity that was checked by the American Revolution; then the long-headed worthies of the Saltmarket took up cotton, and cotton was weighed down by iron, and iron was set afloat as well as wood; and a host of other trades sprang up.

> On Glasgow Green, we are told, James Watt thought of the steam condenser that was the great practical step toward starting such merry-go-roundabouts here at Fair time, and so many wheels on which the progress of the world has spun with such acceleration. If the first model of a steamship was made in Edinburgh, the first passenger paddle-boat that plied in Britain was that between Greenock and Glasgow in 1812. Glasgow, not quite so large as Edinburgh in James Watt's lifetime, had then begun to outstrip the capital, even before she became environed by a wilderness of 'pits and blast furnaces that honeycomb and blacken the earth, and

burn with a red glare throughout the night for many a mile around', where another writer describes daylight showing 'patches of sour-looking grass surrounded by damp stone walls; gaunt buildings soot-begrimed and gloomy; and an ever-increasing blue-grey mist pierced by tall chimneys'. St Kentigern, alias St Mungo, the patron saint of Glasgow, could hardly now identify the site of his hermitage among noisy Clyde ship-yards and busy streets.

The relations between the two chief cities of Scotland have been a little stiff since Glasgow rose so high in the world, as how should a laird of old pedigree, crippled by forfeitures and mortgages, not look askance from his castellated turrets on the spick and span buildings of an upstart millionaire neighbour, the one standing on his name and title, the other on his shrewdness, honesty and strict attention to the business of life.

In spirit and sentiment, too, the two cities have not always seen eye to eye. Edinburgh often showed herself a bit of a Tory, the ladies of the family having even a tenderness for Jacobitism, but Glasgow has always been Whig, with grey homespun for its own wear rather than the tartans it manufactured in the way of business.

Glasgow was also markedly Protestant from an early date. Even in the days when they dealt in rum, the Glasgow folk were noted as sober and sedate, their morals, indeed, being pushed to austerity. Theatrical performances, forbidden under Cromwell's Puritan rule, were here held in horror after they had ceased to be banned in the capital. And as for the Sabbath-keeping that was the sacrament of old Presbyterianism, this is what one record of social life in Scotland in the eighteenth century has to say about Glasgow:

To secure proper observance of the Sabbath, compurgators or 'bumbailies' patrolled the streets on Saturday night to see that by ten o'clock all folk were quietly at home; and if incautious sounds

BROOMIELAW, GLASGOW

betokening untimely revelry issued from behind a door, or a stream of light from chinks of a window-shutter betrayed a jovial company within, they entered and broke up the party which dared to be happy so near the Lord's own day. On Sabbath, as in other towns, the elders, in their turn, perambulated the streets during divine service, and visited the Green in the evening, haling all 'vaguers' to kirk or session. The profound stillness of the Sabbath was preternatural, except when the multitudinous tramp of heavy shoes came from a vast voiceless throng of churchgoers. In these streets of which the patrols 'made a solitude and called it peace', at all other hours no persons passed, no sound was heard, no dog dared bark. In the mirk Sabbath nights no lamp was lit, because all but profane persons were engaged in solemn exercises at home. During the day the window-shutters were, in strict households, just opened enough to let inmates see to walk about the room, or to read the Bible by sitting close to the window-panes.

Times soon changed in Glasgow, where Sunday trams came to be tolerated before they desecrated Edinburgh. By the middle of the nineteenth century one strict minister of Arran was in the habit of warning his flock that they were growing as wicked as Glasgow folk, and almost as bad as them of Edinburgh – the superlative profligacy of London being no doubt taken for granted.

The city of Glasgow neatly divides the river on which it stands into two parts: the lower, broader reaches that stretch down to Greenock and the docks; and the wilder, deeper, more picturesque water that tumbles down from its source in the hills of Lanark and Strathclyde.

In the Middle Ages the whole course of the river was probably deeper and more clearly defined than it is now, for it is recorded that in the reign of Malcolm Canmore in the eleventh century a fleet of 160 ships landed at Renfrew, some six miles below Glasgow, where the river was certainly too narrow to accommodate such an invasion 800 years later. In the twelfth

century shoals of herrings are also known to have penetrated as far as Renfrew, where the monks had a royal charter allowing them to fish.

But by the middle of the seventeenth century the silt of the river at and below Glasgow made it unnavigable to all but the smallest vessels. The local populace had long neglected the commercial potential of the Clyde, viewing it merely as a source of trout and salmon. However, in 1662, the town of Dumbarton expressed its unwillingness to serve as the port of Glasgow, and the Glaswegians had to find other ways of carrying goods between their burgeoning warehouses and the trading ships. It was ordained that 'for the more commodious laidining and landing of boats', a quay be constructed in the city; and there is evidence of the practical Glaswegian approach to the matter in the record a year later of an instruction that oak timber from the cathedral be used to carry out a necessary alteration to the pier.

Despite this reinforcement, the quay had to be replaced at great expense within thirty years – but it was a matter of scant importance, as no ships could come within fourteen miles of it. As late as the 1750s, in the five and a half miles of water that lay between Renfrew and Glasgow, there were no fewer than fourteen shallows, five of which were no more than 18 inches deep at low water. In 1770 an act was passed authorising the deepening of the channel to at least 7 feet, and within a few years one John Colborne of Chester had achieved precisely that. He also succeeded in increasing the tidal flow of the river by dredging, giving Glasgow an 11-foot range between low and high tide where previously the difference had been barely perceptible. So, by the end of the eighteenth century, Glasgow had for the first time the status of a real port.

But developments in shipping meant that these improvements had constantly to be improved upon. Dredging continued to deepen and straighten the river channel. As recently as 1863, ships with draughts of between 14 and 21 feet often ran aground in the river and were forced to wait for high tide before they could move; some even had to be partially unloaded. By the early years

of the twentieth century vessels with a draught of 27 feet could pass freely.

Greenock, on the broadest part of the Clyde, was for a long time a more important port. Here goods were trans-shipped to lighter vessels for the last stage of their journey to Glasgow, and great was the resentment in the larger city of the heavy tolls charged in Greenock for this service. Greenock was also in the early days the home of Scottish ship repairers; there was no 'graving dock' on the Upper Clyde until 1875. But in the later years of the nineteenth century the traffic up the Clyde grew, if not greatly in numbers, then enormously in volume. The 30,000 journeys between Glasgow and Greenock in 1863 represented not much over 3 million tons; by 1906 this figure was over 11 million, while goods in and out had increased sixfold to over 9 million tons.

By that time, too, the port was one of the most cosmopolitan in the world. An account of Glasgow in 1901 includes the following description:

> The liner de luxe, as Liverpool people understand her in the *Oceania* or the *Campania* or the *St Louis*, is not to be seen on the narrow Clyde, and the Cardiff man, accustomed to his miles of coal traders, will find disappointment here; still, if you were to spend a diligent morning in the docks, you will find few types of the British mercantile marine amissing. The Transatlantic passenger steamers of the Allan and Anchor firms; the strange East-Coastish lines of the Donaldson carriers ('lines like a hat-box', as an old shipper had it), the queer-shaped turret ships of the Clan Company, which look as though they had swallowed more cargo than they could digest, the big bright-funnelled South American traders, bristling with derricks and samson-posts; the China Mutual steamers, with their names in the script of far Cathay on their bows; the Loch Line sailing ships, which clip Australian records every season as keen as any 'grey-hound of the Atlantic'; the four-masted Frenchmen from New Caledonia, the

teak-carrier from Rangoon, the auxiliary screw laden with seal oil and skins from Harbour Grace, the nitrite barque from Chile, the City steamers from India and the Persian Gulf – you can find them all. Then there are the squadrons of tramps that thrash from Bilbao to the Clyde with ore and back again with coal; the Italian fruit boats, the stout cross-channel packets, the Highland steamers and top-sail schooners which congregate in the Kingston Dock.

At the same time, the ships built on the Clyde were to be seen wherever a stretch of water was found, from Lake Baikal to the Amazon, cruising with Malayan princes or breaking speed records off the Australian coast. Ferries and paddle-steamers and battleships all bore the name of the Clyde. It was to ship-building what Sheffield was to steel – inseparable, and a source of inexhaustible pride. As one London ship-builder who chose to establish himself in Glasgow put it, 'When you want apples you go to Covent Garden; for ships, you go to the North.'

From Greenock, outgoing ships turn south into the Firth of Clyde and soon out into open sea, but the visitor desirous of a little tranquillity after the bustle of the port can continue north to Gare Loch and Loch Long, and the spit of land between them, where he will come upon the unspoiled village of Rosneath. Here, an inn designed by Princess Louise, a daughter of Queen Victoria who married the Duke of Argyll, is of a piece with the picturesque scenery all around. Tradition rather than history lends the area its romance – here the Scottish patriot William Wallace is said to have carried out some of his more fearless adventures, and here Jeanie Deans, the stalwart heroine of Scott's *Heart of Midlothian*, meets the Duke of Argyll, as a first step in her in her campaign to obtain a pardon for her wronged sister.

Continuing round the Firth, it is worth making landfall on the Isle of Bute, tucked in amongst the many inlets and peninsulas that form this part of the west coast. Although the island boasts stone circles of which little is known but much has been speculated, most of the history of Bute is tied up in the

FERRY INN, ROSNEATH

castle of Rothesay. Said to have been built for the Norse King Magnus Barefoot in 1098, it was surrendered to the Scots, recovered by the Norse, repossessed by the Stuarts, then finally devastated by Cromwell's troops in 1650. Some twenty-five years later the Argylls completed its ruin by setting fire to all that was left. Today its remains stand on a gentle hillock and swans bathe in the moat that once resisted bloody sieges.

A few miles south-east of Glasgow stands another fine ruin, that of Bothwell Castle, redolent with associations with the last, ill-fated husband of Mary Queen of Scots, described by a contemporary historian as a 'glorious, rash and hazardous young man'. Despite professing to be a Protestant, Bothwell was a loyal supporter of Mary of Guise, the French mother of the Queen of Scots. Although he later served his queen – then a widow for the first time – as a Privy Councillor he was clearly a disruptive influence at her court and spent several years in captivity or exile. Recalled by Mary and restored to his honours at the time of her second marriage, to Lord Darnley. he was almost certainly reponsible for the latter's murder, and was subjected to and acquitted by a token trial for the deed. Within two weeks he abducted Mary and carried her off to Dunbar – though there is no evidence that she was an unwilling victim of his schemes. Wed less than a year before, he was quickly divorced and, within three months of the death of Darnley, Bothwell and Mary were married.

This hasty alliance with her husband's murderer turned Mary's nobles against her. She and Bothwell suffered humiliating defeat at the bloodless Battle of Carberry. Mary was captured, deposed in favour of her infant son and spent the last twenty years of her life in prison before finally meeting her death on the decree of her English cousin Elizabeth. Bothwell fled from Carberry to Dunbar, where he took ship and, blown off course, was captured by a Danish warship and taken a prisoner to Bergen in Norway. He died insane in prison some ten years later. He and Mary had spent precisely one month together as man and wife.

Much of the land around Glasgow contains some of the finest and most

famed scenes in Scotland, not least the market town of Lanark, where King David I built a castle (long since vanished) in the twelfth century and the philanthropist David Dale an experimental New Town, with houses and cotton mills, in 1784. New Lanark overlooks the Cora Linn, the most glorious of the Falls of the Clyde, where Coleridge and Wordsworth are said to have debated long and hard whether the epithet 'magnificent', 'beautiful' or 'sublime' best described it. Cora Linn, although only 90 feet high, has been likened to a miniature Niagara. As one writer in the early years of the twentieth century put it:

> Falls in Britain are out of fashion, perhaps since Niagara and Victoria have created a standard that makes our grandest cataracts mere domestic water-taps by comparison; but still the Falls of Clyde have more than a local reputation, and they remain unspoiled, which is more than may be said of Niagara.

Wordsworth, with the ruins of Corehouse Castle in sight as he listened to the water thundering through the gorge, was, as one might expect, more eloquent:

> Lord of the Vale! astounding flood!
> The dullest leaf in this dark wood
>   Quakes conscious of thy power:
>
> The caves reply with hollow moan,
> And vibrates to its central stone
>   Yon time-cemented tower.

Opposite:

BOTHWELL CASTLE

Turner is but the most celebrated of the many who have been moved to record the Falls on canvas – his painting is a masterpiece of colourful fancy, portraying little of the reality of the scene, yet still conveying all this is impressive about it.

Not far from the Falls is one of the prettiest of the Clyde's many tributaries, the Mouse, and within a mile of the point where the two rivers meet is to be found another romantic and impressive spot, the Cartland Crags. The Lake poets visited here, too, but Dorothy Wordsworth dismissed the place as 'rocky dell'. She perhaps did not realise that the chasm in the red and grey rock is the result not of some unexplained violence of the earth, but of the action of the Mouse itself. It is this apparently insignificant creature's constant gnawing over thousands of years that has produced the beautiful and brooding scene. The elegant bridge, said to be Roman, is of course nothing of the sort; but the tale that William Wallace hid himself in one of the caves nearby cannot be dismissed so lightly.

We owe most of what we know about William Wallace to a fifteenth-century minstrel known only as Blind Harry. His work is written with great vigour and, as one critic puts it 'kindles sometimes into poetry'. A fitting tribute, perhaps, not only to this long-dead teller of tales but to the country and the people that are Scotland.

ACKNOWLEDGEMENTS

This book features the work of five artists, whose evocative
pictures captured the grandeur and beauty of Bonnie Scotland, from
her rugged coastline and wild mountain scenery to her fair cities and ports
at the very beginning of the twentieth century. Their work is also
an affectionate and sensitive record of
a rural way of life which was soon
to disappear for ever.

H J Dobson, see pages 71, 75, 97 and 101. J Ayton Symington: see pages 11,
13, 15, 17, 19, 21, 23, 25, 27, 29, 33, 35, 37 39, 41, 43 and 47.
Mary Y Hunter, see frontispiece and page 121, pages 69, 107, 109, 111,
113, 115, 117 and 119. Sutton Palmer, see pages 9, 47, 49, 51,
57, 59, 61, 63 and 123. W M Smith Jr, see pages 53, 55, 65,
67, 73, 77, 79, 81, 83, 85, 87, 89, 91, 93,
95, 99, 103 and 105.

Land of brown heath and shaggy wood,
Land of the mountains and the flood,
Land of my sires! what mortal hand
Can e'er untie the filial band,
That knits me to thy rugged strand!

Walter Scott, Scotland